Explorers!

Ferdinand Magellan

First Explorer Around the World

Arlene Bourgeois Molzahn

Enslow Publishers, Inc.

40 Industrial Road	PO Box 38
Box 398	Aldershot
Berkeley Heights, NJ 07922	Hants GU12 6BP
USA	UK

http://www.enslow.com

With love to my granddaughter Margaret who has
shared so many adventures with me.

Copyright © 2003 Enslow Publishers, Inc.

Library of Congress Cataloging-in-Publication Data

Molzahn, Arlene Bourgeois.
    Ferdinand Magellan, first explorer around the world / Arlene Bourgeois Molzahn.
        p. cm. — (Explorers!)
    Summary: Describes the expedition around the world led by the Portuguese
explorer Ferdinand Magellan.
    Includes bibliographical references (p.   ).
    ISBN 0-7660-2068-1
    1. Magalhães, Fernão de, d. 1521—Journeys—Juvenile literature. 2. Explorers—Portugal—
Biography—Juvenile literature. 3. Voyages around the world—Juvenile literature. [1. Magellan,
Ferdinand, d. 1521. 2. Explorers. 3. Voyages around the world.] I. Title. II. Explorers! (Enslow Publishers)
G286.M2 M65 2003
910'.92—dc21   2002005116

Printed in the United States of America

10 9 8 7 6 5 4 3 2 1

To Our Readers: We have done our best to make sure all Internet Addresses in this book were active and appropriate when we went to press. However, the author and the publisher have no control over and assume no liability for the material available on those Internet sites or on other Web sites they may link to. Any comments or suggestions can be sent by e-mail to comments@enslow.com or to the address on the back cover.

Every effort has been made to locate all copyright holders of material used in this book. If any errors or omissions have occurred, corrections will be made in future editions of this book.

Illustration Credits: © 1999 Artville, LLC., pp. 8 (map), 12, 15, 28; Corel Corporation, pp. 16, 32, 36 (bottom); DigitalVision, pp. 4 (map), 22; Hemera Technologies, Inc. 1997-2000, pp. 6, 37; Library of Congress, pp. 1, 4 (portrait), 8 (portrait), 10, 11, 13, 14, 18, 19, 20, 24, 25, 26, 27, 29, 30, 33, 34, 36 (top), 38, 39, 40.

Cover Illustration: background, Monster Zero Media; portrait, Library of Congress.

Please note: Compasses on the cover and in the book are from © 1999 Artville, LLC.

Contents

List of Maps

★ = starting point

In 1519, Ferdinand Magellan led an expedition around the world. This map shows his starting point and the direction he went.

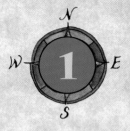

Adventures at Sea

In September 1509, Ferdinand Magellan was on one of five Portuguese ships sailing to the harbor of Malacca. The port city of Malacca, in the country of Malaysia, was in the center of the spice trade. Ships from China, India, Arabia, and the Spice Islands brought silks and spices to the city. The Portuguese planned to capture the city. This would give Portugal control of the Indian Ocean and the spice trade. It would bring many riches to Portugal and to the sailors on the ships that captured Malacca.

When the Portuguese ships reached Malacca, the ruler of the city was very upset. He did not want five warships

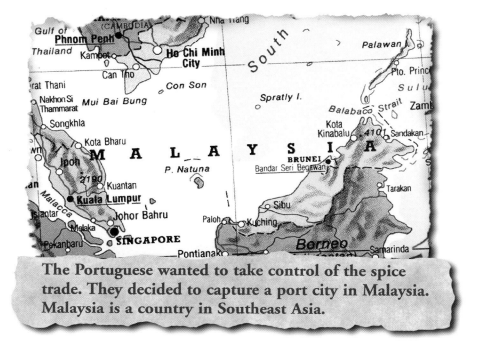

The Portuguese wanted to take control of the spice trade. They decided to capture a port city in Malaysia. Malaysia is a country in Southeast Asia.

docked in his harbor. The ruler had a plan. He was very friendly to the sailors from Portugal. He sent them a friendly greeting, and he invited them to visit his city. Many sailors left the ships to explore the city.

Everything seemed to be fine, but Magellan did not trust the ruler. He stayed on his ship. Then he saw a large number of canoes with men carrying long knives coming toward the ships. He quickly warned the captains of the other Portuguese ships. The sailors that had stayed behind were able to fight off the men from Malacca.

The Portuguese sailors who had gone ashore were also attacked. Most of the men were killed. About forty of them were able to fight off the attackers. These sailors made their way to the pier. Magellan took a small boat, rowed to the pier, and rescued the men. Then the ships safely left Malacca harbor. When he returned to Portugal, Magellan was rewarded for his brave actions. He was given command of his own ship.

Magellan began a life of exciting and dangerous adventures.

Bay of Biscay   France

La Coruña   Pamplona   Barcelona

Valladolid

Portugal   S P A I N   Islas Baleares

Lisbon   Madrid   Valencia

Córdoba   Mediterranean Sea

Sevilla   Granada

Cádiz   Málaga

Strait of Gibraltar

Ferdinand Magellan's name in Portuguese was Fernão de Magalhães. Magellan was born in Portugal around the year 1480.

The Early Years

Ferdinand Magellan was born in a city in the northern part of the country of Portugal. He was the third child of Ruy and Alda Magellan. He had three sisters and a brother. He was born around the year 1480.

Although Magellan's parents were poor, they were nobles. This meant that Magellan and his sisters and brother were sometimes given special treatment. It meant that they would be educated by the king and queen. When Magellan was ten years old, both his parents died.

At the age of twelve, Magellan was sent to Lisbon, the

capital city of Portugal. There he became a page to Queen Leonor. A page may run errands, deliver messages, and sometimes serve as a guide. Magellan went to school at the royal court. He studied geography there. This helped him understand what was known about the world at the time. He learned to sail a ship and he read about the stars and planets. He also learned about the new discoveries made by explorers like Christopher Columbus.

At the age of sixteen, Magellan was made a clerk in an office where sailing expeditions were planned. This office helped buy supplies for ships of the king of Portugal.

Ferdinand Magellan went on his first voyage in March 1505. He went to India and helped set up trading posts

Christopher Columbus sailed in 1492 in search of new lands. He found lands in the Caribbean Sea.

and naval bases. During this voyage, Magellan was hurt in a battle. It took him six months to recover.

At this time in history, many people wanted to find a way to sail to the Indies and the Spice Islands. These countries grew spices like pepper, cloves, cinnamon, and nutmeg. Pepper was used to keep foods from spoiling, and spices were used to hide the taste of spoiled foods. Food spoiled quickly because there was no way to refrigerate it.

People used spices to cover up the tastes of spoiling food. These people are gathering spices.

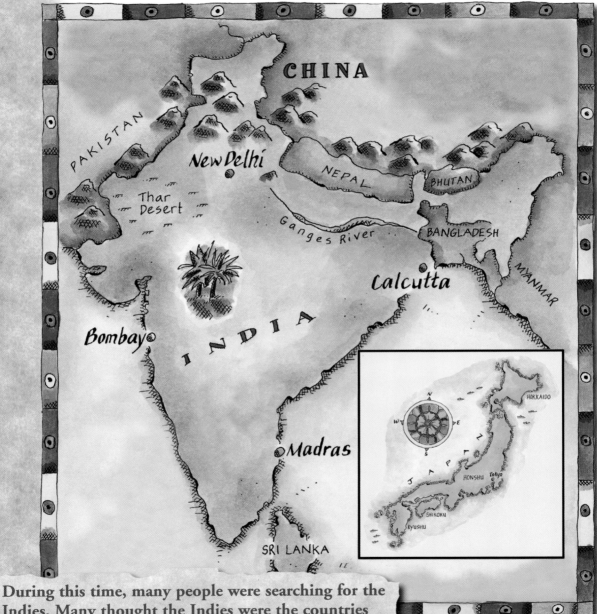

During this time, many people were searching for the Indies. Many thought the Indies were the countries of India, China, and Japan. This is what they look like today.

For many years, spices had been brought to Europe along the same route. The route began by boat over the Red Sea. Next, Arabian merchants brought the spices by camel caravans to Europe. The Arabian merchants guarded this route very well. European traders were not allowed on it. The Arabian merchants kept raising the price of the spices. The price of spices became so high that many people could no longer buy them.

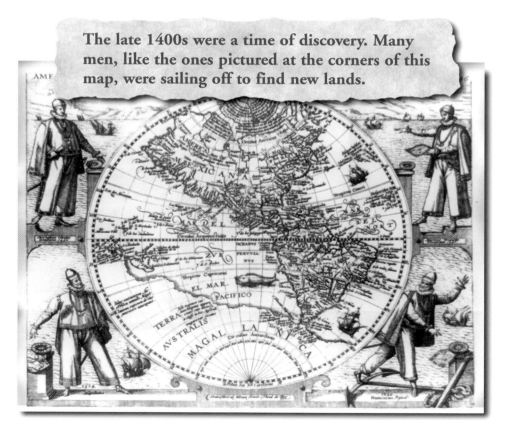

The late 1400s were a time of discovery. Many men, like the ones pictured at the corners of this map, were sailing off to find new lands.

Spain and Portugal sent expeditions along the coast of Africa to find a water route to the Spice Islands. Christopher Columbus claimed to have reached the Indies in 1492 by sailing west on the Great Sea. No one yet knew that Columbus had reached islands in the Caribbean. In 1497, Vasco da Gama sailed around the

Vasco da Gama was another explorer. He sailed to India and returned to Portugal with spices.

VASCO DA GAMA.

southern tip of Africa and reached India. After his second voyage in 1503, da Gama returned to Lisbon, Portugal, with his ship loaded with spices. Portugal soon became the center of the spice trade in Europe.

Ferdinand Magellan had several exciting and dangerous adventures as a sailor. In 1513, he returned to Portugal and joined the army.

Explorers for many countries sailed along the coast of Africa. Spain and Portugal sent ships and men to find a water route to the Spice Islands.

He was badly wounded in 1514 in a battle in Morocco. Because of that wound, he walked with a limp for the rest of his life.

In 1515, Magellan began planning for what would be his greatest adventure.

After many years, Magellan left Portugal and went to Spain (above).

Before the Great Voyage

Magellan had served King Manuel of Portugal for many years. In 1515, Magellan asked the king for three things. First, Magellan wanted more pay for the work he was doing. Next, Magellan asked to be given a different job. Finally, Magellan asked if he could go to another country and serve a different king. The king disliked Magellan and told him he could go wherever he wanted to go and serve any other king.

For a long time Magellan had thought about finding another way to the Spice Islands. He studied maps and read reports from other explorers. By now it was known that Columbus had discovered a new land. But no one in Europe knew the size of this new land. Magellan had a plan. He would sail to the new land and try to find a westward sea passage to the Spice Islands.

King Charles was very interested in Magellan's plan to reach the Spice Islands.

Magellan needed money for ships and men to help him find such an ocean passage. He told a friend, Duarte Barbosa, of his plan. Barbosa invited Magellan to come to Spain and live with him. Barbosa knew King Charles I of Spain. He was sure the king would give Magellan boats and supplies. In October 1517, Magellan left Portugal and went to live with his friend in Spain. Magellan married Barbosa's sister, Beatriz, in December 1517.

Magellan met with eighteen-year-old King Charles of Spain.

Magellan told the king his plan to reach the Spice Islands. He explained how a water route would bring boatloads of riches to Spain. King Charles was very interested.

On March 22, 1518, the king agreed to help Magellan. He gave Magellan and Ruy de Faleira five ships and money. Faleira was a famous astronomer at that time. It was decided that King Charles would get four fifths of anything that was brought back. Magellan would get the rest. Magellan was made commander of the expedition and captain general of the fleet.

Magellan spent the next year getting ready. The five ships he had been

Magellan spent the next year studying maps and globes.

given were small, old, and in poor condition. He had the ships repaired and readied for the voyage. He bou supplies that would be needed.

King Manuel learned of Magellan's plans. If Magellan found another route to the Spice Islands, Portugal would lose money and power. King Manuel sent spies to make

It took a lot of work to get the five ships repaired for the voyage. But after more than a year, Magellan's fleet was ready.

trouble for Magellan. Several of the men who sailed with Magellan were working for King Manuel.

On September 20, 1519, Magellan and his small fleet of ships carrying 277 men began the long journey. Magellan led the expedition from his flagship, the *Trinidad*. The *San Antonio* was the largest ship. It was loaded with food that would be shared by all the ships during the expedition. The other three ships were the *Santiago*, the *Concepción*, and the *Victoria*. The search for a sea passage to the Spice Islands had begun.

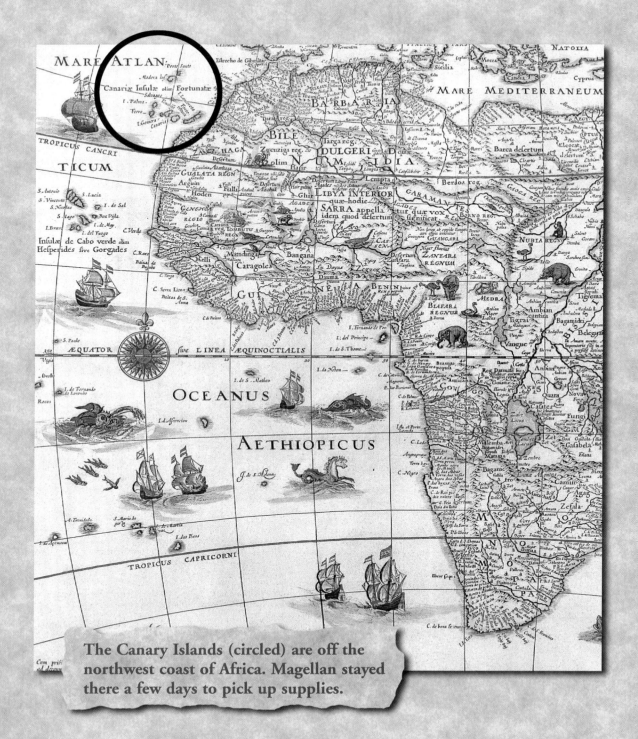

The Canary Islands (circled) are off the northwest coast of Africa. Magellan stayed there a few days to pick up supplies.

Mutiny
on the Ocean

Magellan's five ships headed for the Canary Islands. The Canary Islands are off the northwest coast of Africa. The ships stayed there several days to pick up fresh water and wood. During their stay at the Canary Islands, a ship arrived from Spain. The ship's captain had a letter for Magellan. The letter warned him that three of the Spanish captains planned to take over the expedition. The captains would probably try to kill Magellan. From then on Magellan was on the lookout for trouble.

Magellan did not take the usual route across the ocean. He was afraid that King Manuel would send warships to stop the expedition. Instead of sailing straight across the ocean, Magellan sailed south along the coast of Africa. Here, the ships ran into strong winds.

Finally, the ships got through the stormy seas and headed west for the land that we now call South America. As they neared the equator, the ships sailed into the doldrums. The doldrums is a part of the Atlantic

As the ships sailed near the equator, they sailed into the doldrums. The trip was taking much longer than Magellan had planned. They finally made it to land.

Ocean that is very calm. There is very little wind there. The ships sat almost still in the water. The trip was taking much longer than Magellan had planned.

The Spanish officers on board the ships were angry with Magellan for taking this route. The captain of the *San Antonio* said he would no longer

Some of the men were not happy with Magellan. They tried to start a mutiny, but Magellan stopped it. He put the captain in the brig.

follow Magellan. He wanted the officers of the other ships to agree with him. According to their plan, they would take over Magellan's ship. When Magellan heard of the plot he put the captain in the brig, the jail on the ship. When sailors disagree with their captain and take over the ship, it is called mutiny. Magellan stopped the mutiny. But he feared that this would not be the last time some of the sailors would try to mutiny. A new captain took over the *San Antonio*, and the ships went on.

On December 13, 1519, Magellan's ships arrived at Rio de Janeiro on the coast of South America. The sailors went ashore. For the next two weeks, they traded bells and fishhooks for chickens and fish with the people who lived there.

With fresh water and food on board, the fleet went on to sail south along the coast of South America. They kept searching for a passage to the Spice Islands.

By December 1519, Magellan's expedition headed for South America.

The expedition sailed closer to the South Pole. The weather turned very cold. The sails of the ships were ripped apart by freezing rain and high winds. The men became very tired and unhappy.

By March 31, 1520, the ships had been on the ocean for six months. Magellan steered his fleet to a small harbor. He called the place San Julian. He decided

The explorers went ashore in South America.

to stay there for the winter. (Winter south of the equator is in the months of June, July, and August.) Magellan told his men to go ashore to build huts and hunt for food.

The captains of the *Victoria*, the *Concepción*, and the original captain of the *San Antonio* had a secret meeting the night after the landing. During the night, they took control of their three ships. In the morning they sent a message to Magellan asking him to agree to their terms. If he did, they would return the ships to his command.

Magellan's ships reached the coast of Brazil and landed in Rio de Janeiro in December 1519.

Magellan sent several men with a letter to the captain of the *Victoria*. Secretly, he also sent another boat with men he could trust to the *Victoria*. Fighting broke out and Magellan's men won the fight. The captain of the *Victoria* was killed. Magellan's men quickly took back control of the ship. Then, Magellan's men recaptured the *San Antonio*. Next, Magellan blocked the harbor with the three ships that were loyal to him. This stopped the other two ships from escaping. Magellan had stopped yet another mutiny.

Ships during a battle might have looked like this.

After Magellan discovered a narrow passage from the Atlantic Ocean to the Pacific Ocean (seen here), many of the men wanted to return home.

5

New Lands, New People

Soon after reaching San Julian, Magellan discovered that he had not received all the supplies he had ordered. Portuguese spies had changed the amount and the kinds of goods that were put on the ships. Now there was not enough food. Magellan sent some men out to hunt for food. They found ducks, penguins, and other animals.

Magellan grew tired of waiting for spring to come. In June 1520, he sent the *Santiago* south to explore along the coast. The ship ran into rocks during a storm. Two sailors from the *Santiago* walked sixty miles back to San Julian to get help. Magellan sent a ship to rescue the rest

When food supplies ran low, Magellan's men were able to hunt for penguins.

of the men. Now Magellan had only four ships.

While the fleet wintered at San Julian, the people who lived there visited them. The ship's crew called these people "giants." They were not really giants but were much taller than the sailors. One sailor wrote in his journal that the men were "so tall that the tallest of us only comes up to their waist." The sailors tricked two of these tall people and forced them onto one of the ships. This caused trouble for the expedition, and Magellan and his ships left San Julian. They sailed farther south to a place they named Santa Cruz.

On October 18, 1520, Magellan set sail with his four remaining ships. On November 1, 1520, two of the ships found a narrow passage from the Atlantic Ocean to the Pacific Ocean. Magellan named this passage the Strait of All Saints, after a Christian holy day celebrated November 1. Later it was renamed the Strait of Magellan.

A strait is a narrow passage connecting two large bodies of water. This strait is narrow and rocky. It is about 350 miles long and had many sharp curves. It took the whole month of November for the fleet to sail through the strait. Many of the men wanted to return home now that a passage had been found. But Magellan wanted to reach the Spice Islands.

The *San Antonio* did not continue on the expedition. One night, the ship secretly left the fleet and returned to Spain.

On November 1, 1520, the ships found a narrow passage. Magellan named it the Strait of All Saints, but it was later renamed the Strait of Magellan.

On November 28, 1520, Magellan's three remaining ships left the Strait. The ships sailed into the calm waters of the South Sea. Another explorer, Vasco Núñez de Balboa, had been the first European man to discover these waters in 1513. But it was Magellan who named it. He called it the Peaceful Sea, and today it is called the Pacific Ocean.

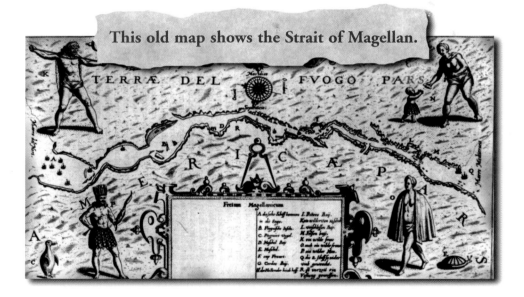

This old map shows the Strait of Magellan.

6

The *Victoria* Comes Home

Magellan did not know the size of the Pacific Ocean. He and his men thought that they would reach the Spice Islands very soon after reaching this ocean. But it was ninety-eight days before the men saw other people again.

The journey across the Pacific was horrible. The *San Antonio* had left with a lot of the dried food. So before leaving the Strait of Magellan, the men packed fresh food on the ships. But soon the fresh food began to spoil, and the drinking water became very stale. The sailors became sick with a disease called scurvy, which is caused by not eating enough vitamin C. Fresh fruits and vegetables have Vitamin C in them. There was no place to get these in the middle of the ocean. Many men died. Others were too sick to work.

On January 24, 1521, the ships stopped at a small island. No one lived there, but the men were able to get a supply of fresh water. On March 5, 1521, the men spotted land again. It was the island that is called Guam today. The men got bananas, coconuts, yams, rice, and fish. This food helped the men get stronger again.

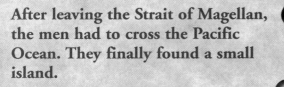

After leaving the Strait of Magellan, the men had to cross the Pacific Ocean. They finally found a small island.

On March 16, Magellan's fleet arrived at another group of islands. Today these islands are called the Philippines. Magellan claimed these new islands for Spain. He wanted to explore many of them before returning home.

Magellan was Christian. He wanted to bring his religion to the people of these islands. His plan was working until he came to the island of Mactan. The chief did not want to

Ferdinand Magellan claimed the islands that we today call the Philippines for Spain.

become Christian. Some of the chief's enemies talked Magellan into attacking the island and forcing the people to become Christians. On April 27, 1521, he led a group of about sixty men and attacked the island. Thousands battled with Magellan's men. The men fought hard and well, but they could not win. Ferdinand Magellan was killed in this battle.

His men returned to their ships, leaving Magellan on

Magellan tried to teach the people who lived on the islands about his religion. They did not like it. A battle started between the people of Mactan and Magellan's men.

the battlefield. They knew they must go on without Magellan. A large number of men had died on the voyage. There were not enough sailors to run the three ships left in the fleet. So the men decided to burn the ship *Concepción*. The *Trinidad* and the *Victoria* continued sailing west.

On November 6, 1521, the two ships finally reached the Spice Islands. The *Trinidad* needed some repairs, so the *Victoria* left first to sail back to Spain. The *Trinidad* was captured by the Portuguese. The sailors were sent to prison and many died.

The *Victoria* sailed across the Indian Ocean and around the tip of Africa on its voyage home. On September 6, 1522, it reached Spain. Of the 277 men in five ships who started out on the voyage, only eighteen men in one ship went all the way around the world

Ferdinand Magellan died in a battle. His men continued the expedition.

This 1544 map shows the route Ferdinand Magellan and his crew sailed. The route is noted by the dark line.

before returning to Spain. The expedition showed that the world's oceans were all connected. After Magellan's journey, explorers and mapmakers had a better idea of the size of the lands and the oceans of the world. The expedition also showed that the world was much larger than anyone had ever imagined.

Magellan did not go all the way around the world, but

his sailors finished the journey. He is remembered as the first person to lead an expedition around the world.

His discovery of the Strait of Magellan let other explorers continue the search for the Spice Islands and new lands.

Timeline

1480—Ferdinand Magellan is born in the northern part of Portugal.

1492—Becomes a page for Queen Leonor in Lisbon, Portugal.

1496—Is made a squire in the service of King Manuel I of Portugal.

1517—Leaves Portugal to live in Spain.

March 22, 1518—King Charles of Spain agrees to pay for Magellan's expedition.

September 20, 1519—The expedition leaves for their trip around the world.

November 1520—The expedition reaches the Pacific Ocean.

1521—Magellan dies in the Philippines.

September 6, 1522—The ship *Victoria* returns to Spain with a crew of eighteen.

Words to Know

astronomer—A person who studies stars and planets.

caravan—A group of vehicles or people traveling together; usually in a line.

continent—A very large body of land. The continents of the world are: Asia, Africa, Europe, North America, South America, Antarctica, and Australia.

doldrums—A place in the ocean near the equator where it is normally very calm.

equator—An imaginary circle around the middle of the earth.

expedition—A journey or voyage taken for a special purpose such as to find something or to learn something.

fleet—A number of ships traveling together.

mutiny—When sailors disagree with their captain and take over their ship.

rescue—To save or free someone or something.

reward—A gift, a present, or some kind of pay for a job well done.

royalty—A king or a queen, or members of their families.

strait—A narrow strip of water connecting two large bodies of water.

voyage—A trip by water from one place to another.

Learn More About
Ferdinand Magellan

Books

Burgan, Michael. *Ferdinand Magellan and the First Trip Around the World*. Minneapolis, Minn.: Compass Point Books, 2001.

Gallagher, Jim. *Ferdinand Magellan and the First Voyage Around the World*. Broomall, Penn.: Chelsea House Publishers, 2000.

Ganeri, Anita. *Ferdinand Magellan*. North Mankato, Minn.: Thameside Press, 1999.

Hurwicz, Claude. *Ferdinand Magellan*. New York: Rosen Publishing Group, 2000.

Hynson, Colin. *Magellan and the Exploration of South America*. New York: Barrons Juveniles, 1998.

Internet Addresses

Zoom Explorers

<http://www.enchantedlearning.com/explorers/>

This is a great site to learn more about Ferdinand Magellan and other great explorers.

Gander Academy Ferdinand Magellan

<http://www.stemnet.nf.ca/CITE/exmagellan.htm>

At this site, you can find a list of Web sites all about Magellan.

Index